SEEING EARTH
FROM SPACE

SEEING EARTH FROM SPACE

PATRICIA LAUBER

· ORCHARD BOOKS ·
New York

Pages 2–3: The Agena Docking Vehicle as seen from Gemini X
against the curvature of Earth.
Page 5: An astronaut sets out on a space walk as the shuttle
glides around the earth. Note Earth's curvature at right.
Page 76: Andros Island, one of the Bahamas, can be seen as part
of a large area of shallow seas, 50 to 250 feet deep and marked
by sand waves built by currents. The dark blue areas are deep
ocean, where the sea floor lies 3,000 feet below the surface.

Text copyright © 1990 by Patricia Lauber

First Orchard Paperbacks edition 1994

All illustrations courtesy of NASA, except the following:
Jacket front and p. 51 courtesy of and copyright by
European Space Agency.
Pages 54–55, 58, 59, courtesy of NOAA/NESDIS.

Orchard Books
95 Madison Avenue
New York, NY 10016

Manufactured in Hong Kong
Printed and bound by Toppan Printing Company, Inc.
Book design by Kathleen Westray

Hardcover   10   9   8   7   6   5   4   3
Paperback   10   9   8   7   6   5   4   3   2

The text of this book is set in 13 point Berkeley Old Style Medium.
The illustrations are full-color photographs.

Library of Congress Cataloging-in-Publication Data
Lauber, Patricia.
Seeing Earth from space / by Patricia Lauber.
p.   cm.   Includes bibliographical references.
Summary: Text and photographs taken from space
depict the nature, evolution, and future of Earth.
ISBN 0-531-05902-2 (tr.) ISBN 0-531-08502-3 (lib. bdg.)
ISBN 0-531-07057-3 (pbk.)
1. Earth—Juvenile literature.   2. Earth sciences—
Juvenile literature.   [1. Earth.]   I. Title.
QB631.4.L38   1990
525—dc20   89-77523

· CONTENTS ·

· PLANET EARTH ·

On their way to the moon, Apollo 8 astronauts looked back and saw a bright blue globe, partly masked by white clouds and set against the black of space. At that moment they became the first people ever to see Earth as a planet. Their photographs and others show us Earth as we can never see it for ourselves. They also show us something we know but find hard to believe: We are all flying through space. Our spaceship is the earth, whirling around the sun at 67,000 miles an hour.

Other new views come from photographs taken by astronauts orbiting a few hundred miles above Earth's surface. These astronauts are too close to see the full face of the earth. But they see large pieces of it at one time, something we cannot do. Trying to see the earth from its surface is like looking at a large painting while standing up against it. We see only details. To see the picture, we must back off.

Astronauts in orbit have backed off from Earth. They see the full length of rivers, the folds of mountains, the birth of hurricanes, the straight lines of roads and bridges that mark the cities of the world. Their photographs give us a space tour of our home planet.

Still different pictures of Earth come from satellites carrying sensors, radar, and other instruments. They show us things that the human eye cannot see for itself.

Together, all these views of Earth teach us much about our planet, whether by showing us the unseen or by taking us sight-seeing with the astronauts.

· SIGHTSEEING ·

The view from space is of the tops of clouds. Thunderheads loom up, sometimes seeming to be set afire by bursts of lightning. At other times jagged streaks of lightning are hurled from cloud to cloud.

Places appear, some as familiar as pages from a geography book—the hook of Cape Cod, the fingers of the Great Lakes, the bird's foot of the Mississippi Delta. The delta is made of sediment—soil and bits of rock—carried by the Mississippi River. As the river meets the Gulf of Mexico and slows, it drops its burden, making the delta grow. Currents carry some of the sediment away to other shores.

Florida seems to be floating in the sea as the rays of the rising sun stream down and the sun itself is reflected in the Gulf of Mexico. The strange shapes in the sky are caused by sunlight reflecting on the window and camera lens. Orbiting at 18,000 miles an hour, astronauts must seize their chances to take photographs. They cannot change their angle or wait till later.

With its snow and ice tinged by the rising sun, part of Kamchatka
Peninsula stretches out from Siberia toward Alaska.

Still other scenes are so strange that they seem un-Earthly. This one looks more like the atmosphere of a giant outer planet than like part of Earth. But the photograph actually shows salt flats and the salt lake of a windblown desert in Iran.

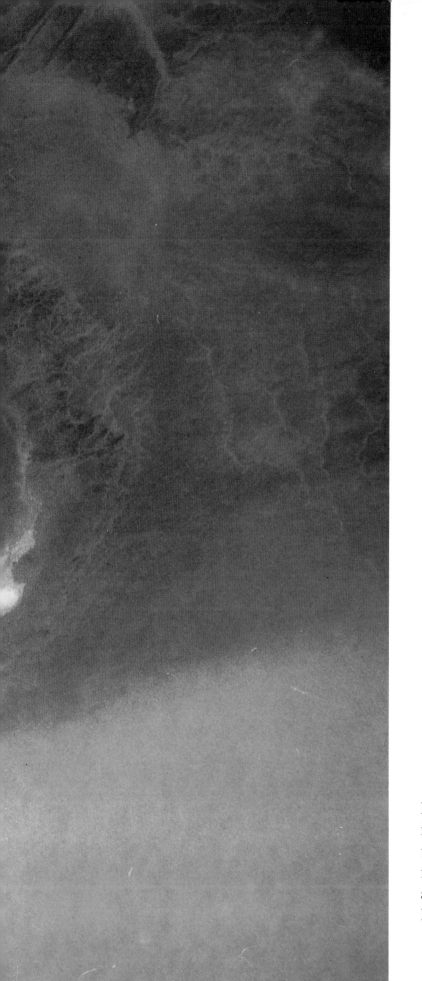

Long ago, earth scientists think, flat rock was forced up here into the shape of a dome. Over time the roof of the dome was worn away, leaving rings of rock within rings of rock. The rings are in the part of the Sahara Desert that lies in Mauritania.

The color of Lake Natron in Tanzania surprised the shuttle crew who flew over it. Experts later said the color was caused by drying salts, blooms of algae, and perhaps by the tens of thousands of pink flamingos that feed on the algae. The lake lies in a valley known as the East African Rift. It is a place where the earth's crust is being torn apart as molten rock rises from inside the earth.

Astronauts sometimes look down at giant storms, such as the eye of Typhoon Pat over the Pacific.

They also see signs of human activities that worry them. This golden haze over the Indian Ocean near Madagascar is not natural but man-made, a sign of air pollution. The sun is glinting off smoke particles in the air.

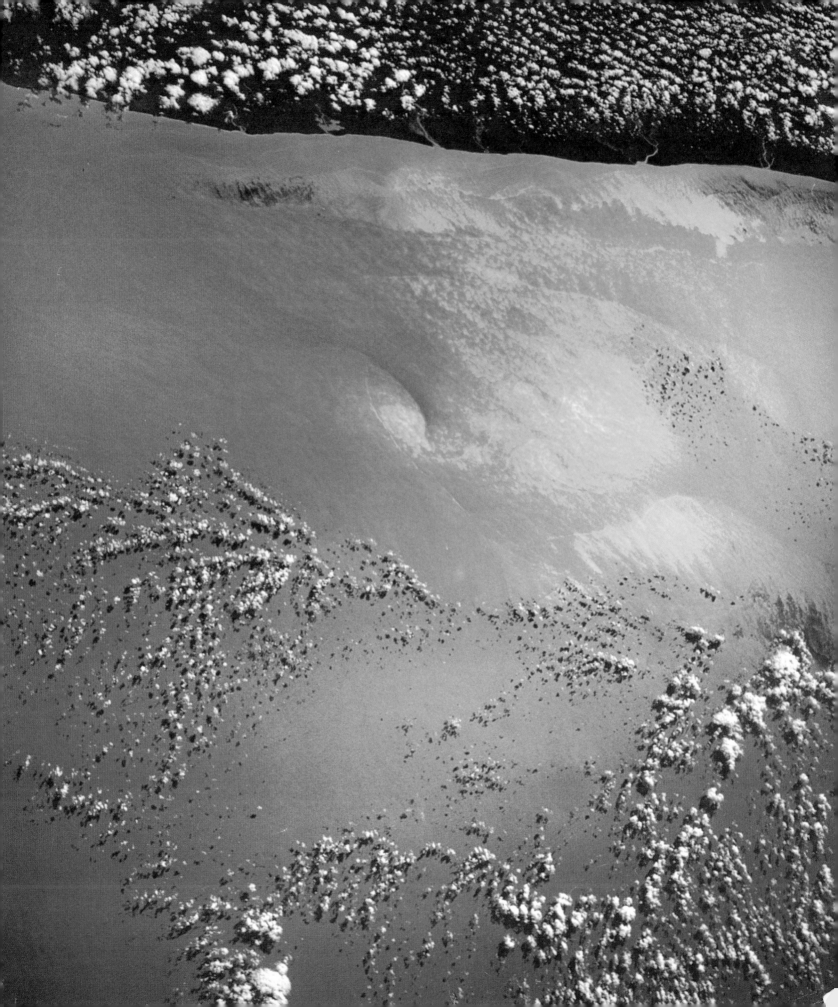

Islands glide by, tiny outposts in the seas that cover two thirds of Earth. Most of them grew from undersea volcanoes. Eruptions built mountains so high that they broke through the surface of the sea and became islands.

Once an island is born, life arrives. Seeds and plants wash up on its shores. Insects and seeds arrive on the winds. Birds find the island, bringing more seeds in their feathers and on their feet. In time the island may become a place where people can live and which they settle. That is what happened with this island, Santa Cruz de Tenerife, which is one of the Canary Islands, in the Atlantic Ocean. At its center, with a light dusting of snow, is Tiedi, an inactive volcano.

The Hawaiian Islands were also built by undersea volcanoes. The big island of Hawaii was originally two islands, one built by the volcano Mauna Loa, the other by Mauna Kea. Huge lava flows from Mauna Loa linked the two islands and made them one. The clouds in this photograph are moving from right to left. Those to the left were disturbed and broken up as they passed over the islands.

Bora-Bora, center in the picture at left, is a Pacific island that is changing. The middle of the island was built by a volcano. Where the shores of the island shelved off into the ocean, the waters were warm and shallow. Here colonies of corals took hold. Each coral was a tiny animal with a hard skeleton on the outside of its body. At first corals attached themselves to rocks, later to the skeletons of earlier generations. As time passed, they formed a reef around the island. The photograph shows the reef, as well as the lagoon that circles the island, inside the reef. Now the volcano is cold and dead. It is slowly sinking back into the earth. In time it will disappear, leaving a ring of coral and sand with a lagoon at the center. The ring of coral will be the kind of island called an atoll. The same thing is happening to the islands of Raiatea and Tahaa (lower right). Tapai (upper left) has already become an atoll.

The islands of Tarawa (partly cloud-covered) and Abaiang, shown below, also became atolls many years ago.

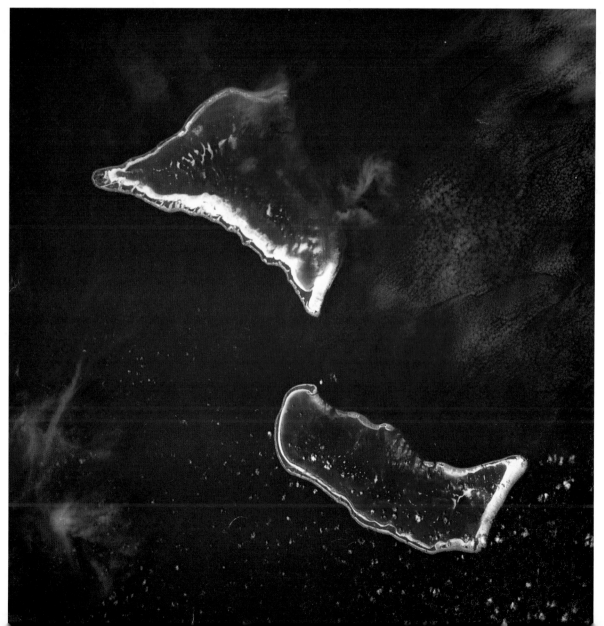

The earth's crust is broken into huge pieces, or plates, that are in motion. Moving at a rate of an inch or two a year, they carry along whatever is on top of them—ocean floor, islands, whole continents. Millions of years ago, the plate carrying India collided with the plate carrying Asia. When the two land masses were pressed together, the Himalaya Mountains began to crumple out of the crust. As the plates went on pressing together, the mountains grew taller and taller. Today they are still among the earth's young, growing mountains, and their folded, tilted rock tells of an ancient, great collision.

The Manicouagan Ring in Quebec is a sign of a different kind of collision. It is the scar left by a huge meteorite that crashed into the earth, perhaps 210 million years ago. Today a dam has turned part of the crater into a reservoir.

When Earth and the other planets were young, such collisions were common. The signs of them are clear on the pockmarked faces of the moon and Mercury, where little erosion takes place; without atmosphere and water there is no wind or rain to wear away the scars. On Earth some signs of collisions are hidden by the oceans. Others have weathered away or been destroyed by movements of Earth's crust. Scientists wonder how these giant collisions have affected life on Earth. Some think that 65 million years ago the earth collided with a giant meteorite or swarm of meteorites. The collision hurled so much dust into the air that the sun's light was cut off for weeks. Without sunlight, green plants died, then plant-eating animals, then animals that ate other animals. And that, they think, is why the dinosaurs died out, along with many other kinds of life.

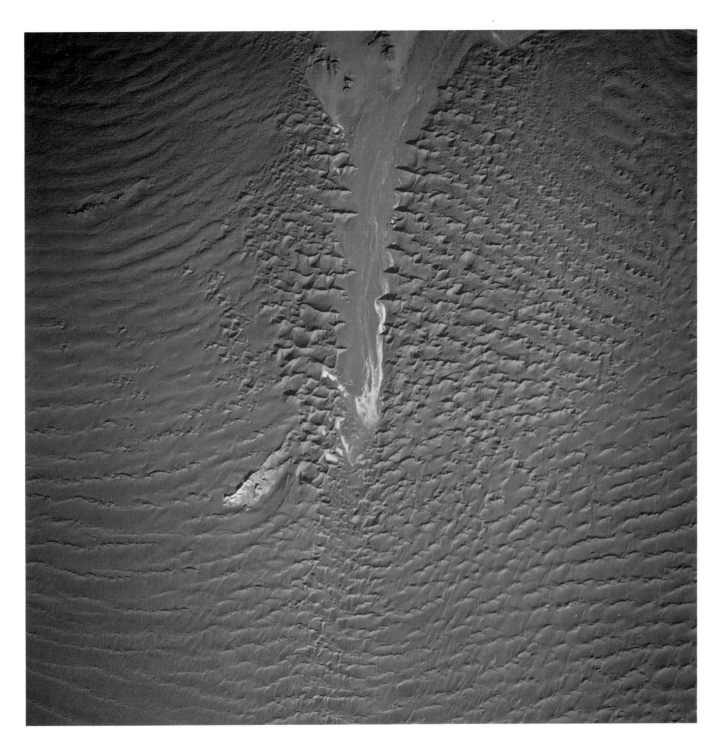

Shifting, trackless sands make deserts difficult, and often dangerous, to explore by land. From space, huge areas of them can be seen at a time. This is the Namib Desert, which is part of Namibia, on the west coast of Africa. Its dunes are the biggest on Earth, 2 miles wide and 1,000 feet high. They run for 500 miles, down to the border of South Africa. In the photograph the dunes end sharply at a streambed. From time to time, water flows along the bed, and over the years it has cut a path through the dunes.

Seen from land, one desert may seem much like another. Seen from above, each desert shows its own dune patterns—Algeria's Tifernine Dunes are different from the dunes of the Namib Desert. The dark area shows the volcanoes of the Tademait Plateau and a region that has been thrust upward.

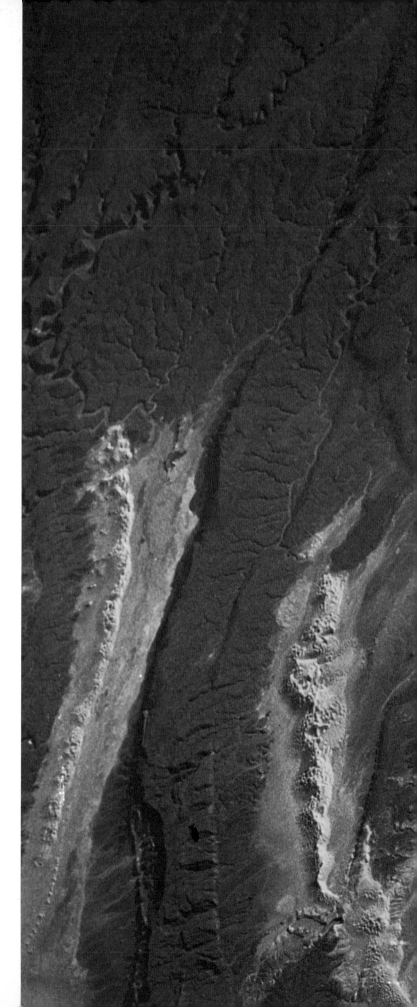

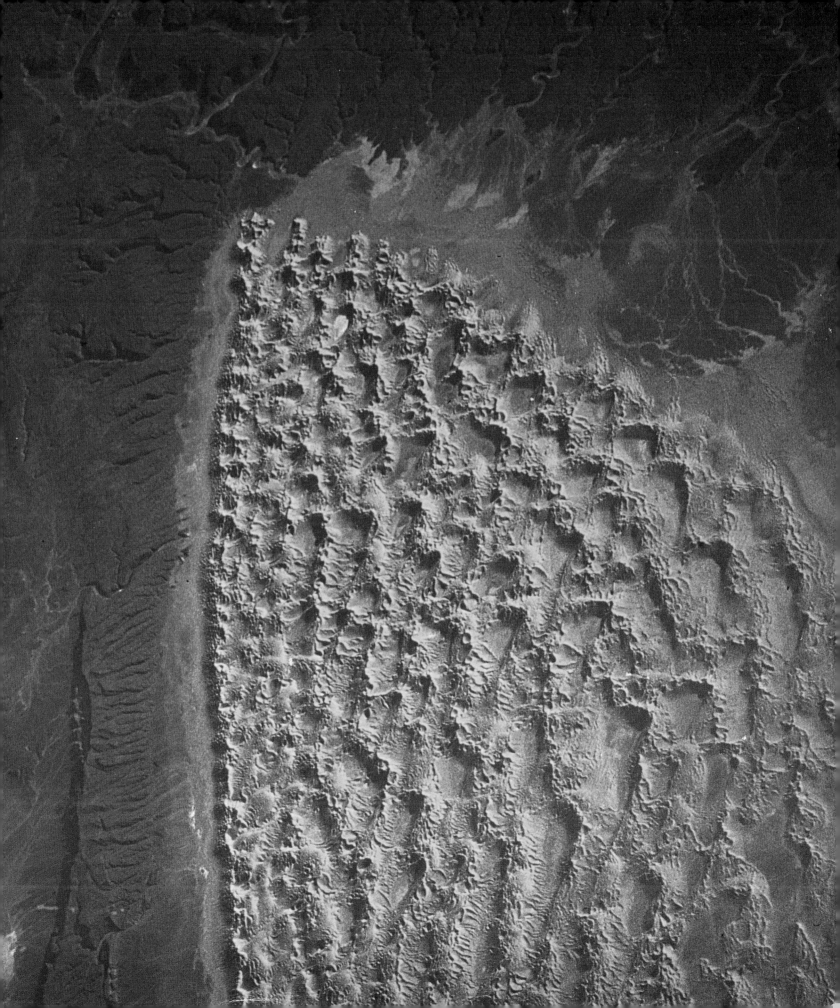

The Tifernine Dunes, in turn, do not look like the Erg (sand desert) Chech in south-western Algeria. In this harsh desert, where no one lives, the dunes are parallel, about 100 miles long, and 5 to 10 miles apart.

Photographs from space give us an overview that helps us to understand our planet. But we also learn from instruments that sense the land, the sea, and the atmosphere. Like space photography, they are all forms of what is called remote sensing.

· REMOTE SENSING ·

Space photography is called remote sensing because it is a way of learning about a target, such as the earth, without touching it. There are many kinds of remote sensing. Among them are ones found in the human body. You use yours every day of your life.

Is a radiator hot? To find out, you don't touch it. You hold your hands out toward it. If there is heat, nerve endings in your skin will sense it. That is one kind of human remote sensing.

Eyesight, or vision, is a much more important kind. To use it, you need light.

White light is a mixture of colors. You see this when the sun's white light breaks up into a band of colors and makes a rainbow in the sky. You see it when white light passes through a prism. The light breaks up into a band of colors known as a spectrum.

Light travels in waves, and each color has its own wavelength. When the sun's white light shines on a buttercup, the flower absorbs most of the wavelengths, but it reflects the yellow ones. And so you see a yellow flower. A purple plum is reflecting a mixture of red and violet wavelengths. A brown dog is reflecting a mixture of red, orange, and yellow ones.

Like the human eye, a camera takes in reflected light. Used with black-and-white or color film, a camera records the kinds of things that the eye sees.

Red wavelengths are the longest that the human eye can detect. So red is the last color we see in the spectrum. But there is color beyond red, color with longer wavelengths. It is in the part of the spectrum called the infrared, meaning "below red." If we could see in the infrared, we would see color beyond red in every rainbow, color we cannot even imagine.

If we could detect even longer infrared wavelengths, we would see something else. After sunset, we would see a dim glow, the glow of heat being given off.

Sunlight warms the earth's surface by day. The heat is absorbed by oceans, deserts, rocks, trees, and everything else on the surface. Some of the heat is radiated back into the atmosphere as infrared energy. If we could see these infrared wavelengths, the landscape would glow at night.

Although human eyes cannot sense infrared, there are ways of detecting it. One is to use film that senses infrared. There are also electronic sensors that detect infrared. They are carried on satellites—the Landsat series launched by the United States and satellites launched by other countries. The sensors scan the earth beneath them. They measure the light reflected by the earth, both the wavelengths we see and the infrared. The sensors are another kind of remote sensing.

Sensors record their measurements as numbers, using a scale of 0 to 255. The numbers are radioed to Earth, where computers put them together and make pictures. Bright false colors are added to make details stand out and to let us see what was recorded in infrared.

Some of the pictures, or images, look like photographs; some don't. But all provide far more information than the eye alone could do.

This Landsat picture was made using information sensed and recorded in green, red, and infrared wavelengths. It shows California's Salton Sea, which looks like a big footprint, and the Imperial Valley, which stretches southward. In the valley's warm, dry climate crops grow year-round, irrigated with water from the Colorado River. Healthy green plants reflect infrared strongly; they appear as bright red in this false-color image. Thinner vegetation is pink. Clear water is black. Windblown sand from the neighboring desert is white. The checkerboard pattern shows that some fields have ripening crops (red and pink) and some are lying fallow, or resting (blue-gray).

Because of a difference in the way farming is done, the border between the United States and Mexico appears as a straight line across the Imperial Valley. It is one of the few national boundaries on Earth that can be seen from space.

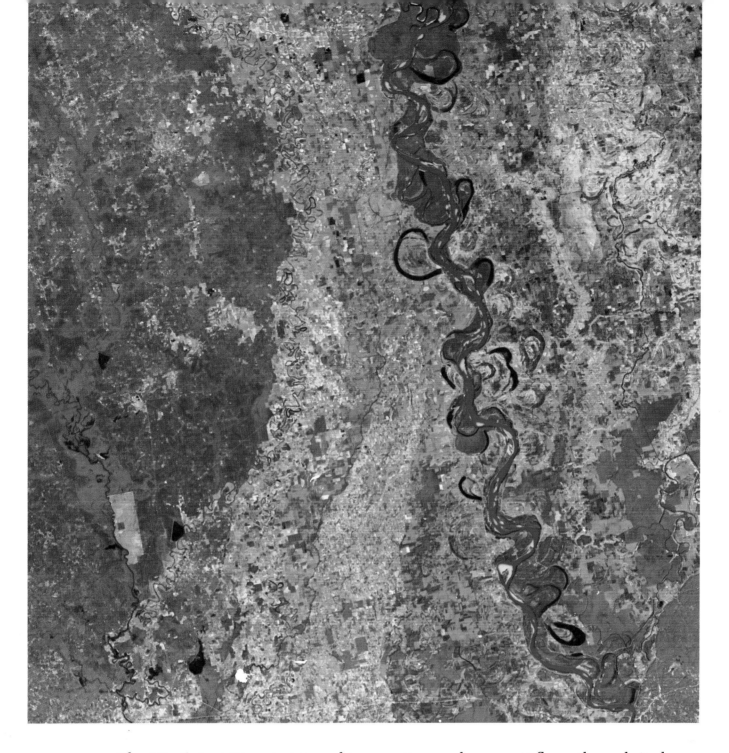

The Mississippi River twists and turns—it meanders—as it flows through its lower valley toward the Gulf of Mexico. Sometimes it changes course, leaving behind the loop- and crescent-shaped lakes that now mark its earlier paths. Because of its meanderings, the lower Mississippi is longer than its valley. It travels one-and-a-half times the length of the valley from Cairo, Illinois, to New Orleans.

In this false-color image the flood plain of the river appears pinkish. Much of it is covered with farms that raise cotton, soybeans, rice, wheat, and oats. On bluffs along the borders of the flood plain, forests of oak, hickory, and pine grow.

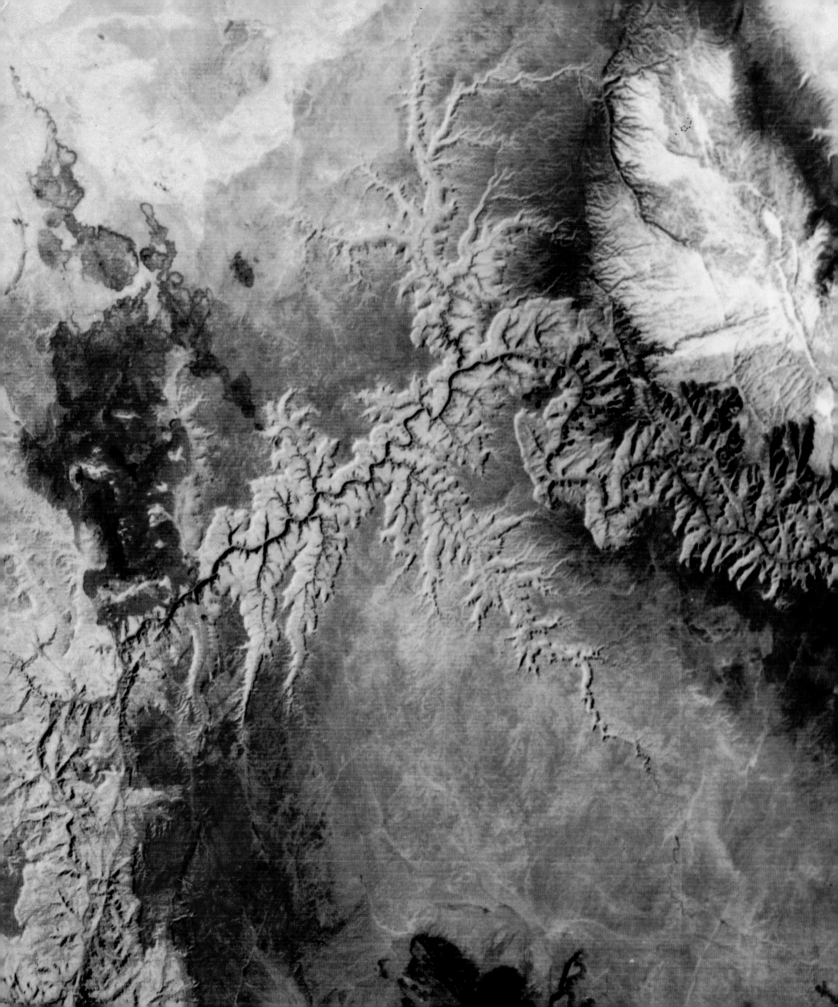

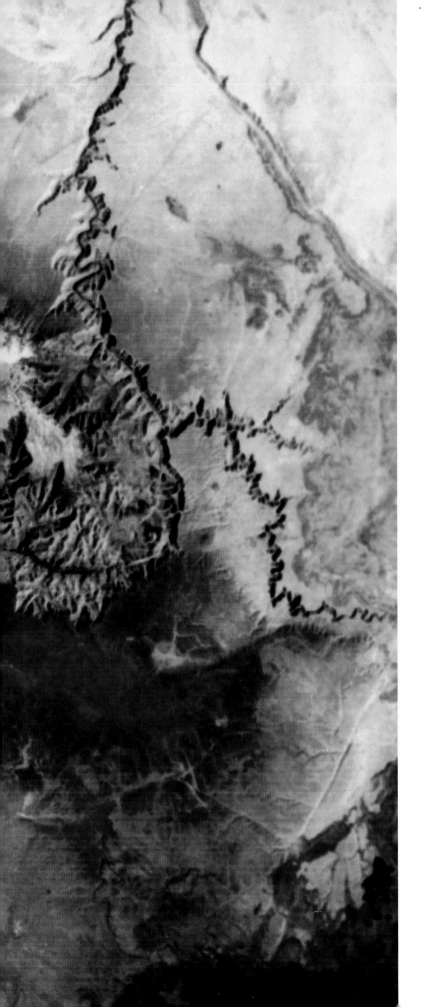

Looking like a scar on the face of the earth, the Grand Canyon twists its way across Arizona in this Landsat picture. This part of the canyon is about a mile deep and 12 miles wide from rim to rim. Its layered rock walls reveal some 2 billion years of Earth's history. The racing Colorado River, which carves the canyon deeper and deeper, is later stopped and pooled by Hoover Dam and Lake Mead.

Radar is still another kind of remote sensing. Unlike the Landsat sensors, it does not measure light reflected from the earth. Instead, it sends out its own radio waves and microwaves. It beams them toward its target and detects their echoes. The strength of the echoes is recorded and used to make maps or pictures. Because it does not use light, radar works both day and night. And because its waves pass through clouds, it can be used when skies are overcast.

One of the space shuttles flew over Montreal, Quebec, at a time when most of the city was covered by clouds. Information from its radar was used to make this false-color image. The St. Lawrence River, at right, is shown in black, as are the smaller rivers. You can see the bridges that cross them. Buildings and pavements appear pink and blue. Land that is being cultivated is dark green. Plant life that grows wild is lighter green. The big green oval to the left of the St. Lawrence is Mount Royal.

The same shuttle flew over the high plateau of northern Peru (below). Its radar showed these folded, layered rocks, some 70 million years old. False colors have been used to highlight different kinds of rock. The wormlike black line in the center of the picture is a river that feeds into the Amazon.

Remote sensing shows us the earth in new and often surprising images. For scientists who use the images, they open up ways of studying the earth that have never existed before.

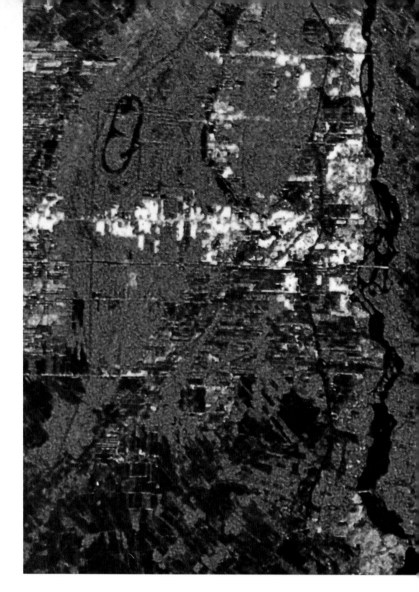

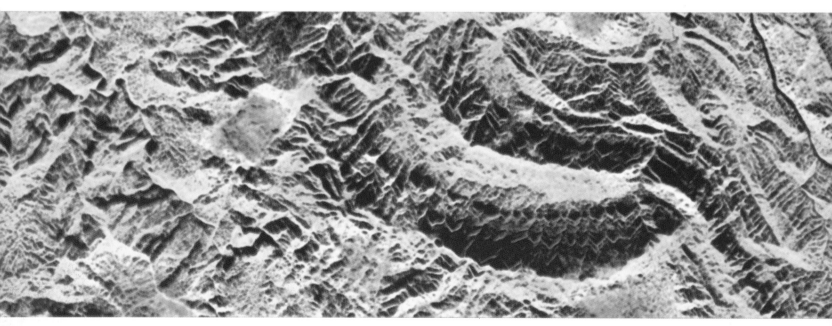

· USING REMOTE SENSING ·

As it orbits, a satellite regularly passes over the same parts of Earth. And so its images let scientists trace what happens as the seasons change. They can, for example, predict flooding by studying winter snowfalls and spring meltings. And they can make cloud-free pictures of any region by piecing together images from different times of year. That was how they obtained this false-color image of Italy. In it, plant life appears in shades of red. Cities and barren areas are blue-gray. Mountains stand out clearly. And the volcano Mount Etna, its sides dark with lava, can be seen on the island of Sicily, off the toe of the boot.

The view from space helps many kinds of scientists. Geographers have discovered mountains and lakes that did not appear on their maps. They have found a previously unknown island off the coast of Labrador and a reef in the Indian Ocean. They have mapped mountain ranges, deserts, and Arctic lands.

In earlier times, oceanographers could only study the oceans from ships. It was long, slow work. The oceans were huge, covering more than 70 percent of Earth's surface, and the ships were small. Now these scientists can also study the oceans through pictures from space. They can see large features that they could not see from ships. They can track currents, such as the Gulf Stream, that play a major part in climate. They can track the masses of tiny plants that form the base of food chains in the oceans. They can see and follow details in ways that used to be impossible.

They can, for example, follow the swirling rings of water thrown off by currents, such as these eddies in the Mediterranean Sea. Eddies can be 200 miles in diameter and travel hundreds of miles over several years. By stirring up the water, eddies speed up the spread of heat from tropical areas. They are also important to the life of the sea, because they carry minerals used by plants in making their food.

Seasat was a United States satellite that failed after a few months. It was designed to study the oceans—roughness, the patterns of currents, water temperature, the speed of surface winds, sea ice. One of its instruments was a radar altimeter, which measured the height of the satellite above the ocean. Seasat sent out a beam of radio waves. When they hit the surface of the water, they were reflected back to the altimeter and recorded.

The results were a surprise: The surface of the ocean rises and falls with the rise and fall of the seabed beneath it. If you could smooth out all the waves, you would see that the ocean surface has hills and valleys. They mark places where there are undersea mountains and trenches. Where there is a big seamount, for example, there

is extra gravity. The seamount pulls a little extra water toward itself. The extra water makes a gentle hill a few feet high. Above a valley or a trench, there is a dip in the surface. And so a map of the ocean surface is also a map of the ocean floor.

This map shows several deep ocean trenches. They are places where plates of the earth's crust are colliding. The leading edge of one plate slides under the other and turns down, creating a trench.

The map also shows the Mid-Atlantic Ridge, a range of undersea volcanic mountains. The range runs down the middle of the Atlantic Ocean and continues around the world, like the seam on a baseball. Here molten rock wells up from inside the earth and is added to the trailing edges of plates.

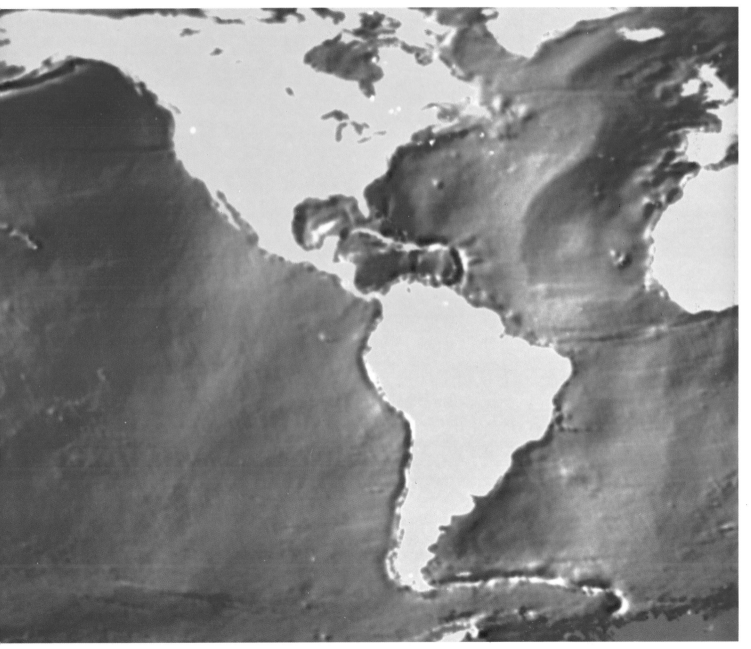

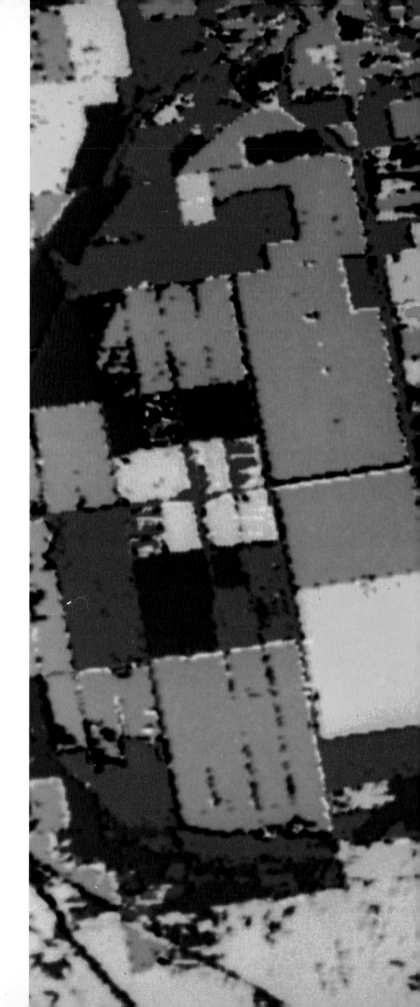

In many Landsat images all thick, healthy plant life appears bright red, while thinner vegetation is lighter. But images can also be used to find out what kind of plants are growing. Every kind of plant reflects sunlight in its own way; it has its own place in the spectrum, which is called its spectral signature. A spectral signature is like a fingerprint. Just as no two people have the same fingerprints, so no two kinds of plant have the same spectral signature. Plant scientists have learned the signature of oats, for example, by studying images of fields where they know oats are growing. When they find the same signature in another place, it tells them the crop is oats. A different signature tells them the crop is wheat. By giving each signature a false color, they can see which fields are planted to oats and which are planted to wheat. In this image of the San Joaquin Valley in California, fields of cotton are red. Yellow shows safflower, while dark green shows wheat stubble. Fields lying fallow are blue.

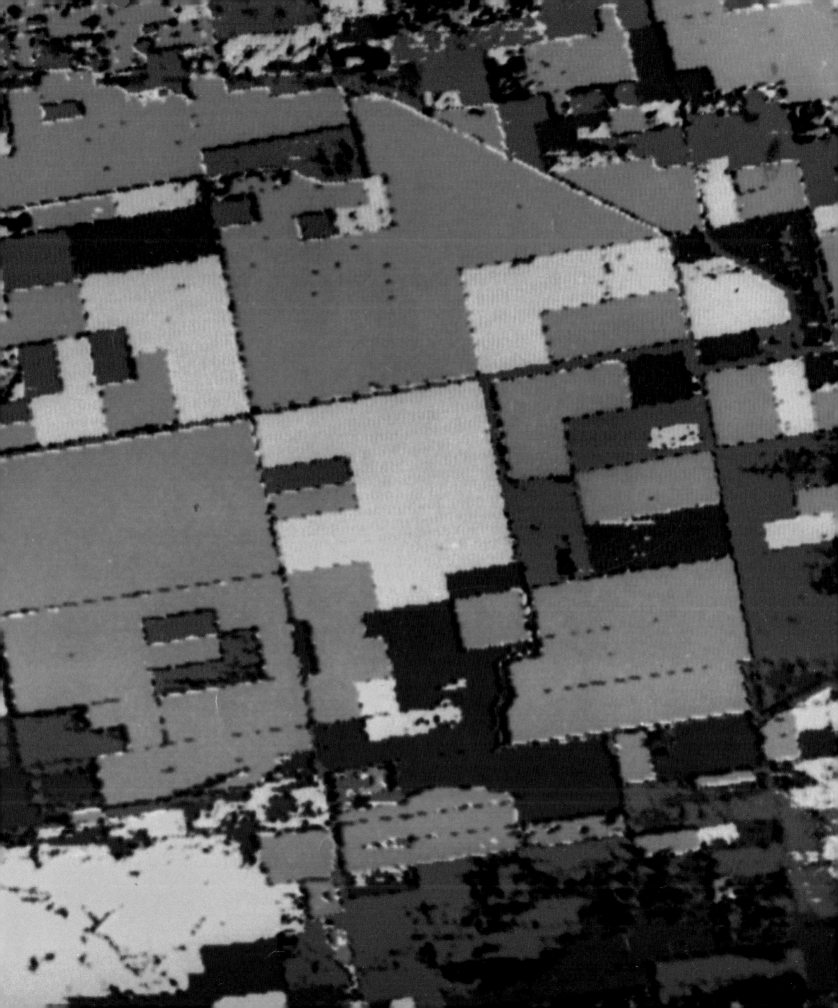

Shuttle astronauts photographed this strange scene while passing over the Saudi Arabian desert. The pattern of perfect circles told them they were seeing something man-made. It turned out to be farmland. Each circle marked a piece of desert irrigated by a sprinkler that pumped water from underground and broadcast it in a circle.

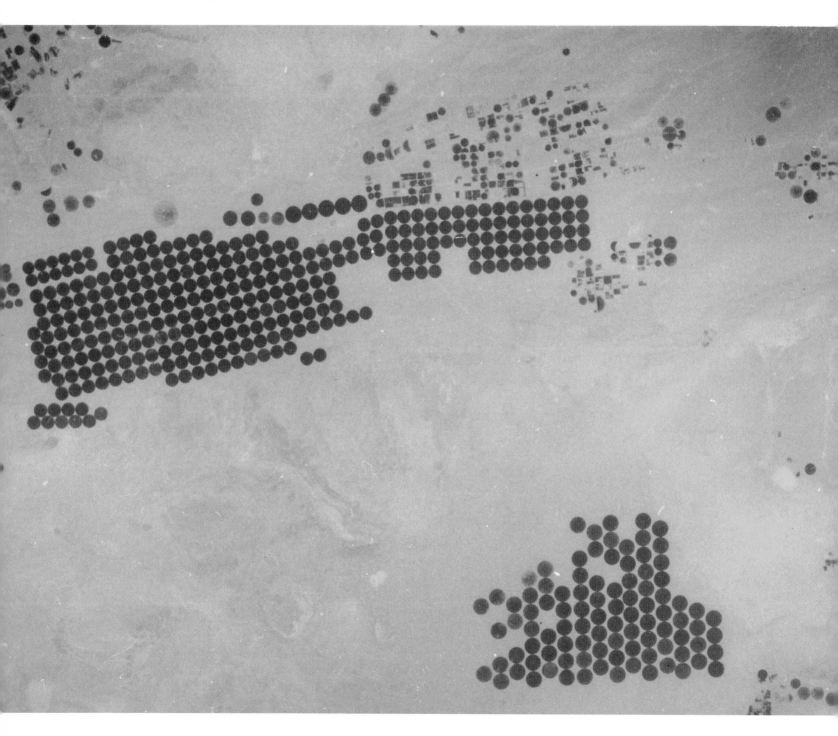

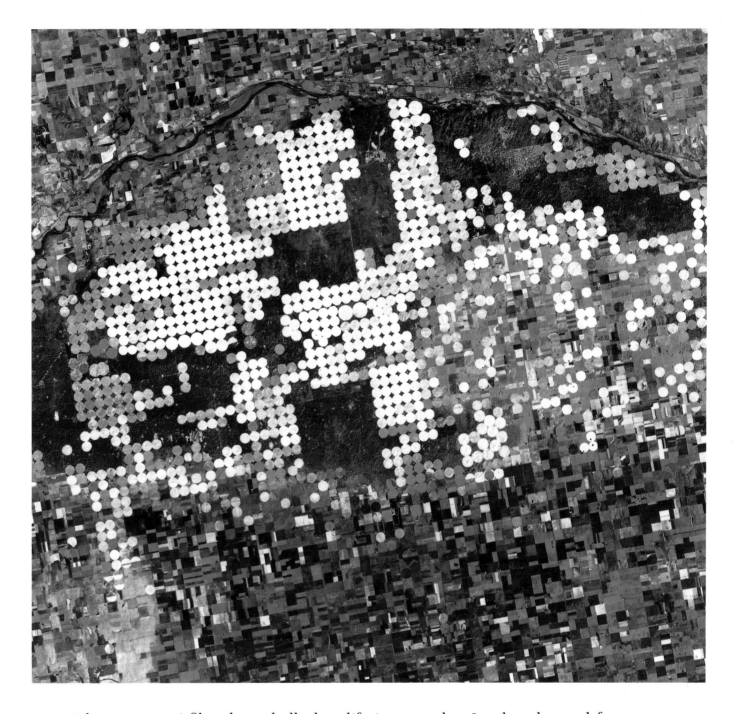

The astronauts' film showed all plant life in one color. Landsat detected far more when it passed over Garden City, Kansas. Here, too, are the circles that tell how the crops are watered. But the Landsat image also tells what the crops are. The time of year is December. White shows where corn has been harvested and its stubble left on the ground. Red shows that healthy winter wheat is growing. Fields that are black and white have been left fallow to build moisture in the soil.

By noting small differences in spectral signatures, plant scientists can tell a newly planted crop from a ripe crop. They can tell whether plants are healthy. They can even tell if unhealthy plants are suffering from a disease or being attacked by pests.

Geologists use images from space to study places that are far away or hard to explore by land. The image on this page shows Death Valley in southeastern California. It is the lowest point in the Americas, dropping 282 feet below sea level, and the driest, hottest part of the United States. The false-color image shows that almost no plants grow in the region. Red appears only on top of the Panamint Mountains (shown in the left half of this picture), where a forest grows, and in a few small spots where crops can be irrigated. The image also shows the courses of streams that sometimes run down the slopes of the Panamint Mountains, spread out into fans, and drop the sediment that they were carrying.

Using images from space, geologists have discovered faults in the earth's crust—long cracks that mark places where earthquakes may occur. These are places where dams, power plants, pipelines, factories, and houses should not be built. Geologists also use images to search for minerals. Sometimes they look for the kind of landforms where oil, for example, is likely to be found. Sometimes they look for traces of minerals at the surface. Just as each kind of plant has its own spectral signature, so does each kind of mineral. Seen in the infrared, sandstone is different from shale, tin from copper. With the help of such clues, geologists have discovered copper, nickel, zinc, and uranium in the United States, tin in Brazil, copper in Mexico.

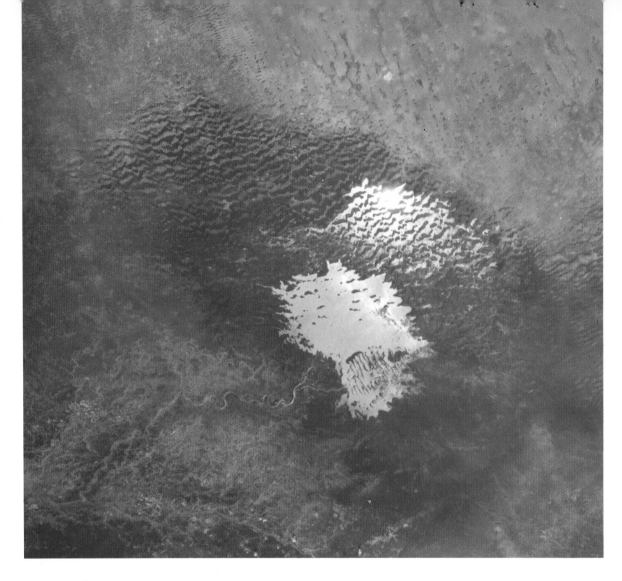

Scientists who study droughts and food supplies use images from space to track changes. Astronaut photographs, for example, show the effect of drought in northern Africa, where the rains have failed year after year. Lake Chad, in Chad and Nigeria, is a once-giant body of water. When first photographed from space, it covered about 7,000 square miles. In this photograph, taken twenty years later, it has shrunk to 1,000 square miles. Ancient dunes, long covered by lake waters, can now be seen. They appear both as dunes and as islands.

The growth of the Sahara Desert along its southern edge can also be traced. Here too the rains have failed, year after year. But the greater problem is that the land cannot support the number of people who live on it. Farmers till poorer and poorer land. They do not let fields lie fallow and rest. They fell trees for firewood or building materials, and without trees to hold the soil in place, winds carry it away. Cattle, goats, and camels strip the land of low-growing plants. The exposed soil bakes hard in the sun and loses its ability to take in and store water. When rain does come, water runs off quickly or evaporates. Sand blows in and buries the plants that remain. And so dry lands become desert—and are added to the Sahara.

Today the Sahara is the world's largest desert. But this part of North Africa has not always been dry. It has been a place where rains fell, rivers flowed, plants grew, and animals and people could live. Scientists have known this for a number of years, but an unexpected piece of evidence came to light from shuttle radar.

In 1981 the shuttle Columbia was passing over a region of the Sahara where rain falls about once every fifty years. Its radar passed through several feet of loose, dry sand and echoed off bedrock. Images showed a network of ancient riverbeds, some wider than today's Nile. The find was of great interest to archeologists, scientists who study ancient civilizations and peoples. Several expeditions set out overland and dug down to the riverbeds. They found shells of a land snail that can live only in a moist, tropical climate. They found stones shaped into points at one end, which may have been used as axes or weapons or for hunting. By dating their finds, scientists have discovered three periods when people lived in these river valleys: 212,000, 141,000, and 45,000 years ago.

The picture shows a radar image of the riverbed placed on a Landsat image of the Sahara.

Orbiting high above the earth, weather satellites send back many kinds of information. They use television cameras to photograph clouds, which are a key to understanding weather systems. They measure temperature and moisture in the atmosphere, air pressure, rainfall, snow depth. They report the birth of hurricanes and typhoons in distant parts of the oceans. They track ocean currents that warm or cool land areas. This view from space, together with astronaut photographs, lets weather scientists see weather in the making and weather as it is happening.

The coast of northern California is known for its clouds and fog. They occur when warm moist sea air meets cold water welling up along the coast. The moisture in the air is chilled and condenses into banks of clouds and fog. Here they are about to roll over the peninsula on which San Francisco lies.

A glance is all you need to see that the weather was clear over most of Africa and Europe when this image was returned. Natural color has been added to a black-and-white image produced by Meteosat, a European weather satellite.

Tropical storm Xina, north of Hawaii, is gathering strength, drawing a long trail of clouds into its spiraling center. In the northern hemisphere, hurricanes and other tropical storms spiral counterclockwise.

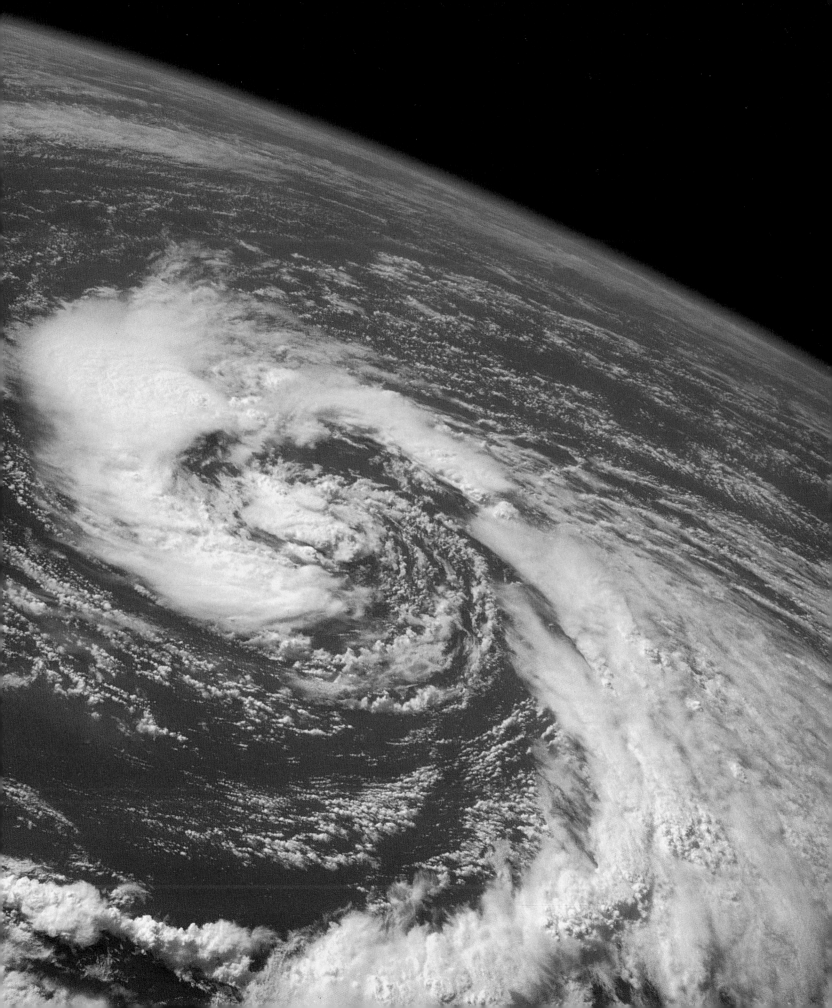

(KELUIN) 192 5   213 5   234 5   255 5   276 5   297 5

Once there was only one way to study the inside of a hurricane: fly an airplane into the heart of the storm. Now weather satellites report on hurricanes, making many kinds of measurements. One kind, shown here, is of temperatures within the storm clouds, using sensors that record infrared heat. The left-hand image shows Hurricane Alicia in

natural color. The right-hand one shows temperatures, measured in degrees Kelvin. (Kelvin is a scale often used by scientists instead of Celsius. The scale starts at absolute zero, the point at which no heat is given off, and goes up. In Kelvin the freezing point of water is 273 degrees, the boiling point, 373 degrees.)

Weather satellites measure the amount of water in the atmosphere over the oceans. The measurements tell weather scientists how much water is evaporating out of the oceans and how much is falling into the oceans as rain. The black ocean areas on this map have very dry air, with no clouds and low humidity. The dark blue are somewhat drier than the light blue, with few clouds. The light areas off western

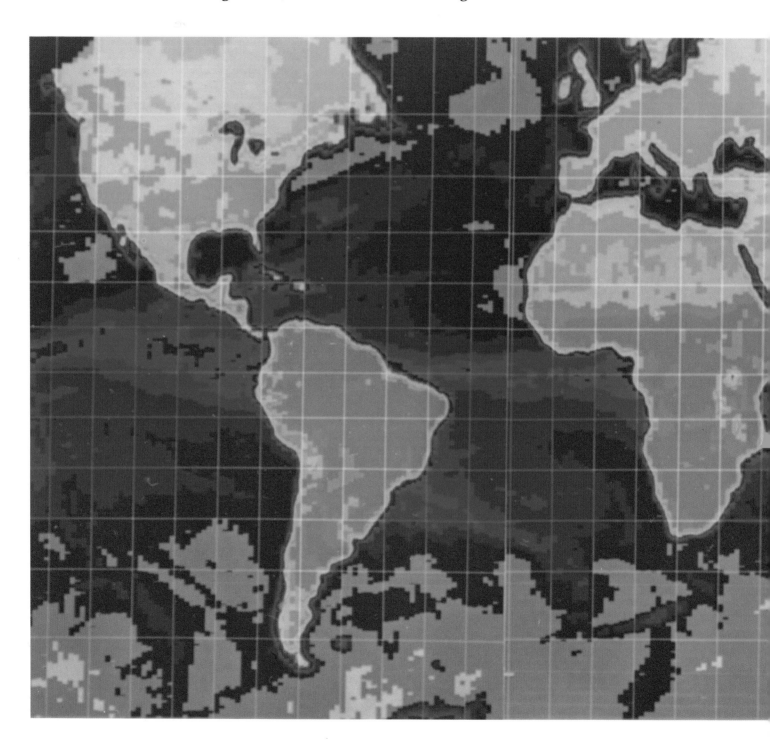

Mexico and the west coast of Africa are a sign of fair skies and sunny weather. The land colors show temperature differences—it is summer in the southern hemisphere and winter in the northern. The brownish colors show that much of the United States and Europe are having mild January weather. The sharp line across Africa marks the end of the dry desert air and the start of thick plant life.

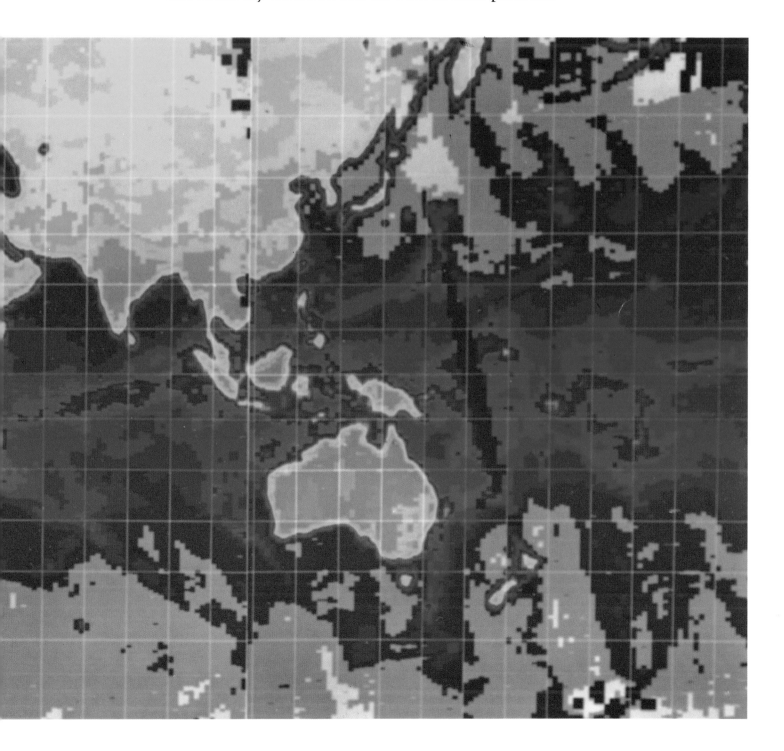

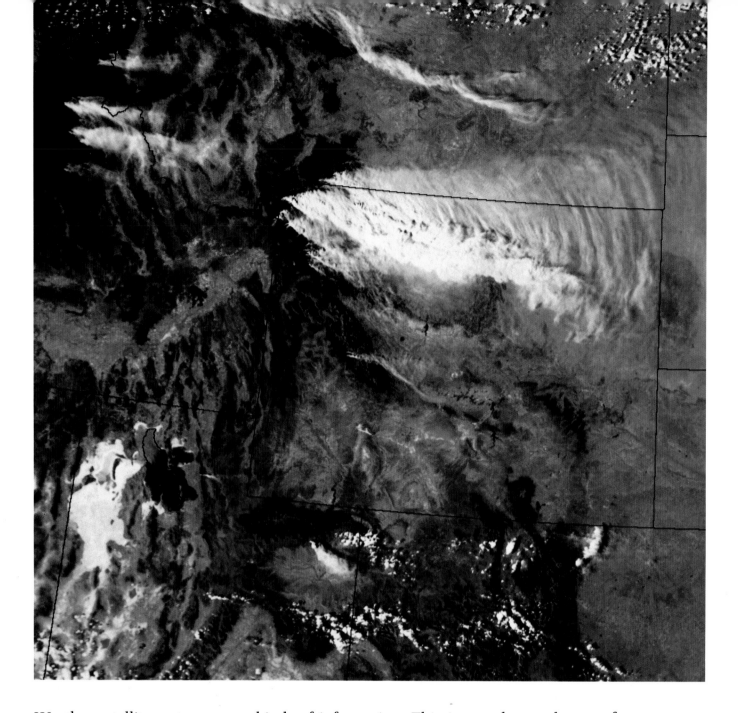

Weather satellites return many kinds of information. This image shows plumes of smoke from the fires that raged in Yellowstone National Park in the summer of 1988.

The same satellites also track wildlife, picking up signals from small radio transmitters attached to the animals. Wildlife biologists track elephants as they move from one country to another. They follow the travels of gray whales and can even tell how deep the whales dive. They track polar bears, musk oxen, and caribou in Alaska and can tell whether the animals are on the move, standing still, or lying down. This is one way biologists learn how human activities are affecting wildlife on Alaska's North Slope, where oil and gas wells have been drilled.

In October 1987 a gigantic iceberg known as B-9 broke away from Antarctica. A weather satellite sent back this view of it. Although the berg looks small, it was 90 miles long and 22 miles wide—twice the area of Rhode Island—and 750 feet deep.

Like all icebergs, B-9 was made of water that came from the sea—that evaporated out, formed clouds, and fell as snow on polar lands. There, over thousands of years, great snows pile up. Under the weight of new snow, the old packs down into ice. In places the ice is hundreds or thousands of feet thick. Because it is under great pressure, the ice flows. It flows toward the sea. From time to time, pieces of it break off and float away as icebergs. As the bergs melt, water is returned to the oceans.

B-9 was just one of five giant icebergs that broke off Antarctica in a period of two years. The amount of ice in it was equal to half the snow that falls on Antarctica in a year. After B-9 crashed into the sea, ocean levels all over the world rose by the thickness of ten playing cards.

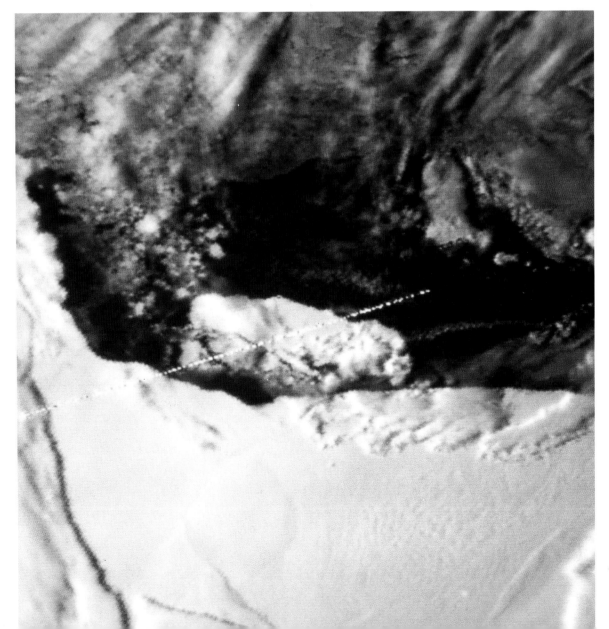

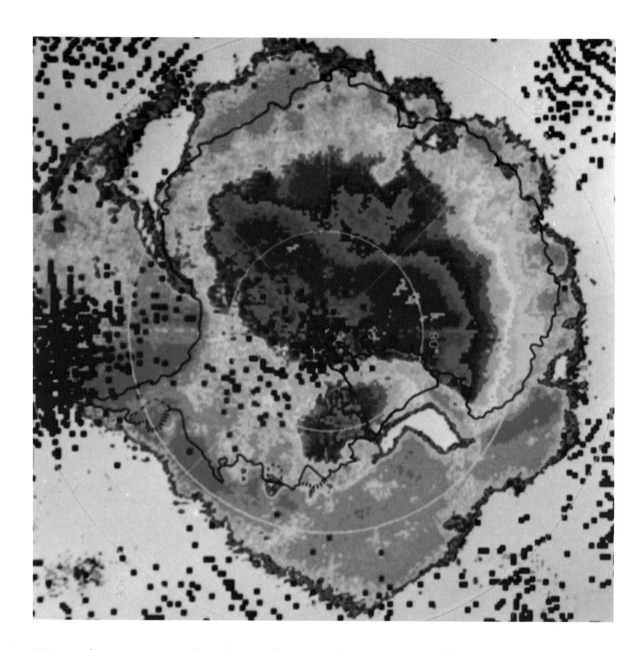

Water also returns to the oceans during polar summers, when snow and ice melt. Scientists can track the amount of melting with images from weather satellites. These two pictures show the big changes that took place over six weeks of an Antarctic summer. (The black spots are gaps in the information received from the satellite.)

The amount of summer melting is one clue to what is happening to the earth's big ice—whether it is growing, shrinking, or staying the same. The size and number of icebergs is another clue. Together they tell something about the amount of water being locked up on land as ice each year and the amount that goes back into the oceans. If the two are about the same, then ocean levels stay the same. If they are not the same, ocean levels change. A changing level is a sign of a change in Earth's

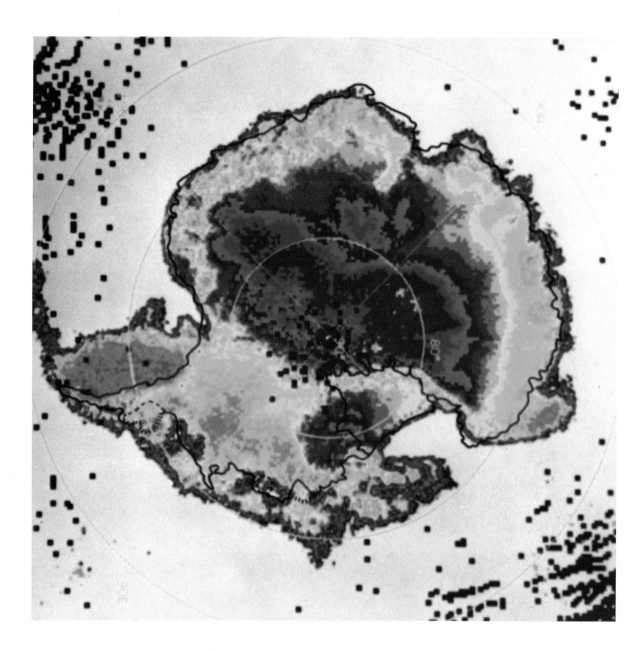

climate. And that is why polar land ice is of interest to scientists who study climate.

There have been times in the past when Earth's climate was cooler and even more water was locked up as land ice. Then ocean levels fell. New coasts appeared along the edges of continents, and former coasts became inland areas.

There have also been times when the earth's climate was warmer and much of the big ice melted. Ocean levels rose. Coastlines disappeared beneath the rising seas, as did low-lying islands.

What is happening now? How much ice is melting and breaking off? Are the big bergs from Antarctica a sign of short-term change or long-term change? That is what scientists would like to find out.

Scientists are also studying the Arctic. Here too water from the oceans is locked up on land as ice. Is the land ice growing, shrinking, or staying the same? Are temperatures changing? How much sea ice is there each winter? One way to find out is to measure temperature over a number of years. To do that scientists use satellite images, such as the one on the facing page. It has the North Pole at its center, with North America at the lower left and Europe at the lower right. Temperatures of mid-January are color coded in degrees Kelvin.

The changes of the past took place naturally and slowly, over hundreds or thousands of years. Plant and animal life had time to adapt, to spread or move. Today many scientists worry that human activities are speeding up natural change. They think that Earth's climate is warming because of what they call the greenhouse effect.

A greenhouse is warmer than the outdoors because it traps some of the sun's heat. The rays pass freely through the glass and into the greenhouse. Plants and other material absorb the heat. After a while they begin to give it off as infrared. Infrared wavelengths do not pass freely through glass, and so heat is trapped in the greenhouse.

Earth's atmosphere acts like the glass in a greenhouse. Sunlight passes through it and warms the earth. The earth radiates infrared heat back into the atmosphere. Some of the heat escapes, but much is trapped. Certain gases in the atmosphere tend to absorb infrared heat. The atmosphere and the earth are warmed. Without the greenhouse effect, the infrared heat would pass through the atmosphere and be lost to space. On Earth, the oceans would be solid ice.

The chief gas in the greenhouse effect is carbon dioxide. In modern times it has been increasing in the atmosphere. Carbon dioxide is released as people burn coal, oil, and natural gas in power plants, factories, homes, and cars and trucks. It is also released when African farmers burn off thousands of square miles of grasslands each year. It is released when tropical rain forests are burned.

Each year, when the dry season arrives, man-made fires rage in the Amazon basin of Brazil. Until satellites began sending back images no one realized how widespread the fires were.

Fires are started by ranchers clearing forests to make grazing land. They are started by settlers, poor people who are desperate for land to grow food. Like the ranchers, they cut down forests and set fire to the fallen trees. But the forest soil is not suited to crops. After two or three years, the settlers start over. They move on, clear more forests, and burn the trees.

≥282.5
280K
275K
270K
265K
260K
255K
250K
245K
240K
235K
230K
225K
220K
215K
210K
205K
200K
195K
190K
185K
180K
175K
170K
165K
160K
155K
150K
145K
140K
135K
<132.5

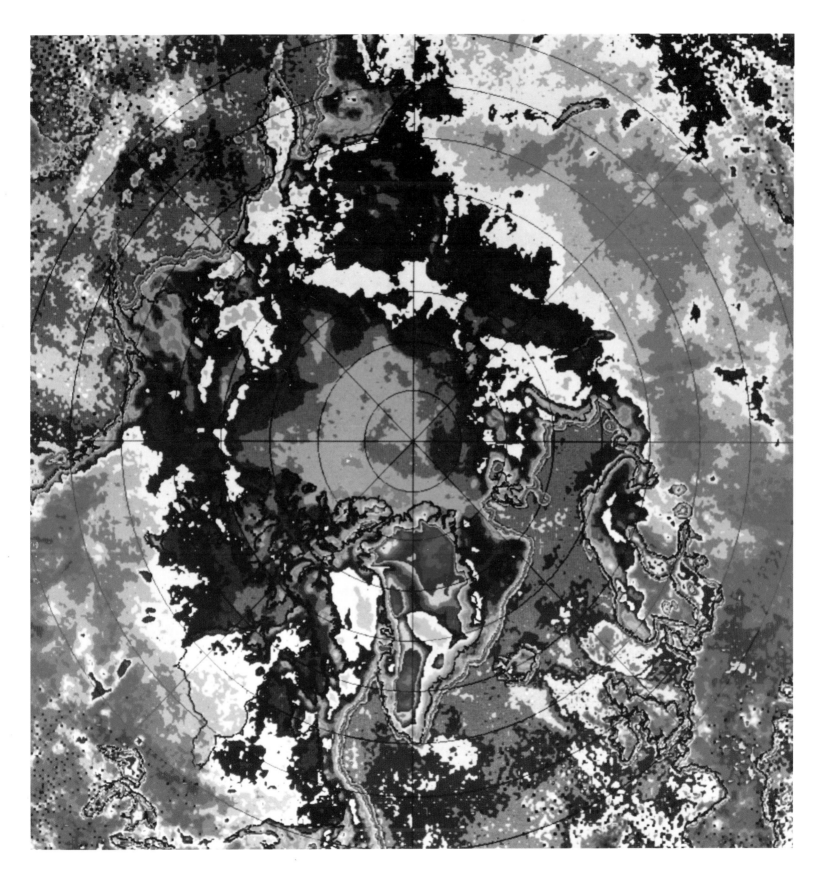

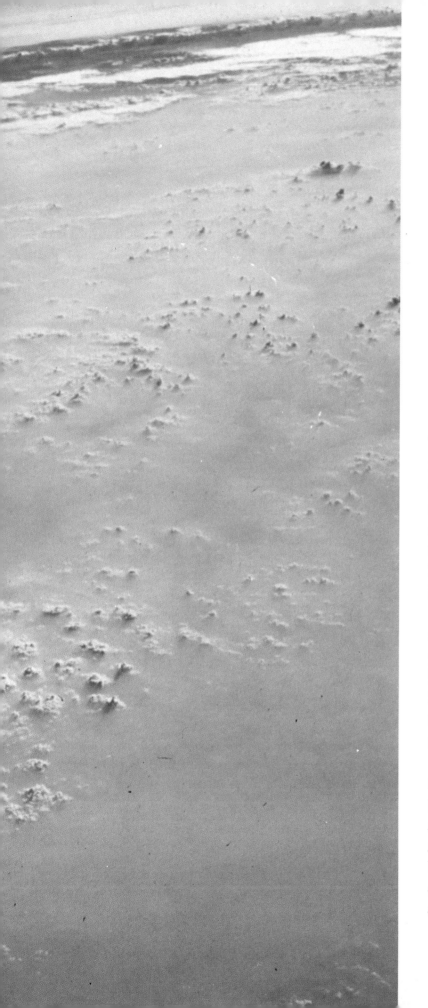

The burning trees send huge clouds of smoke into the air. When shuttle astronauts passed over Brazil in September 1988, the smoke was so thick they could not see the ground. The smoke cloud was so big that it covered an area three times the size of Texas. This photograph looks across the smoke toward the Andes Mountains, about 700 miles away.

Scientists say at least one tenth of all the carbon dioxide added to the atmosphere each year comes from Brazil's part of the Amazon basin. And with each square mile of forest that is felled, the earth loses a square mile of trees that took carbon dioxide out of the atmosphere and used it in making their food.

Human beings are adding large amounts of carbon dioxide to the atmosphere. Some is taken out and stored in green plants. Some is stored in the oceans and in rock, such as limestone. But no one knows for sure how much is being stored. Many scientists worry that more of the sun's heat is being trapped—and the earth is warming.

A warmer Earth would mean more melting of the ice on polar land and rising sea levels. Coastal areas around the world could be in serious trouble.

Hurricanes draw their energy from the ocean's heat. Warming oceans would mean more hurricanes and stronger ones.

Higher temperatures and ocean levels would cause changes in weather patterns. Searing heat and drought might come to regions that now produce much of the world's grain.

For all these reasons, scientists and government leaders are searching for ways to cut back on the greenhouse gases we are adding to the atmosphere. They are looking for ways to burn less fuel. They are trying to help people make a living without destroying forests.

Scientists who study the atmosphere are also concerned about other man-made changes in it. In the earth's upper atmosphere, for example, there is a region called the ozone layer. Ozone is a gas that makes up only a small part of the atmosphere, but that small part is extremely important. It shields the earth from most of the sun's ultraviolet rays.

Small amounts of ultraviolet give people a tan—or a sunburn. Too much ultraviolet can cause skin cancer, eye damage, or other health problems in people and animals. It can also harm crops and life in the oceans. And so scientists were alarmed to discover that the ozone layer above Antarctica was thinning out every spring. It thins so much that scientists speak of a hole in the ozone.

Satellite images, such as those on the facing page, show that the springtime hole changes its shape and position from year to year. The ozone hole (shades of purple) was bigger in 1985 and 1987 than in 1986 and 1988. In the odd-numbered years it covered nearly the entire continent of Antarctica. The dense amounts of ozone (red, orange, and white) were much larger in even-numbered years.

What was happening? Scientists raced to find the answers. As they worked they discovered more bad news. They found a smaller hole over the Arctic. They found that the ozone layer had thinned somewhat all over the globe. And in 1989 they found another giant hole growing rapidly over the Antarctic.

The thinning of the ozone layer seems to have several causes. Some are natural. Others are man-made. Gases and chemicals given off by the burning of fuels and rain forests play a part in thinning the ozone layer. But the chief cause appears to be a group of gases called chlorofluorocarbons (CFCs). These gases are made of chlorine, fluorine, and carbon.

CFCs have been widely used for years to cool coils in refrigerators and air conditioners, to make spray cans work, to make foam for packaging and insulation, and to clean electronic parts. Millions of tons of CFCs escape into the atmosphere from

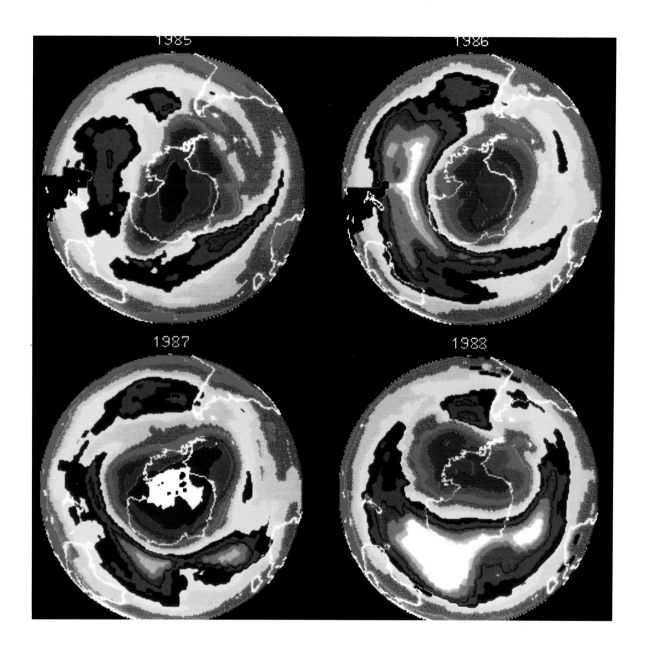

these uses. The gases rise into the upper atmosphere, where they are broken up by ultraviolet radiation. Chlorine atoms are freed and they destroy ozone.

The United States has banned many uses of CFCs. Today a number of countries are working to cut back their use of the gases. They are trying to find other gases that can do the jobs CFCs now do. Their aim is to protect the ozone layer that shields the earth from harmful radiation.

The ability to see Earth from space helps scientists to understand both how the planet works and how human activities are affecting the earth. It helps all of us to share the feelings of the men and women who have gone into space.

· SPACESHIP EARTH ·

The Apollo astronauts who landed on the moon found themselves in a strange new world. No one had walked this ground before; the only footprints were their own. Nowhere was there a trace of life other than their own, only craters, seas of hardened lava, hills, and rocks. Above them stars and planets shone with a brilliance never seen on Earth, for the moon has no atmosphere to dim their light. Yet for the astronauts the most exciting sight was Earth. It was more than home.

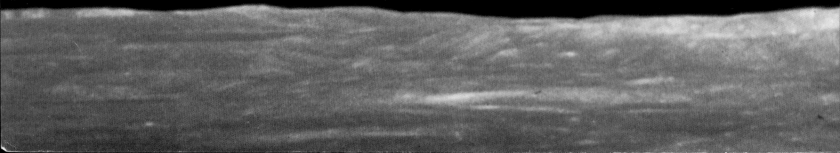

All the men and women who have flown in space—Americans, Soviets, foreign guests—have been awed by the beauty of the earth. They have also been surprised by its size. To a person standing on its surface, the earth appears both large and sturdy. From space it seems small and fragile.

These men and women are often concerned by the man-made changes they see on the earth. They look down at the island of Madagascar (below), where tropical forests are being felled. They see that the ocean around it is red-brown, colored by soil eroding from land without trees and carried to the sea by rivers.

They look down and see the slick of an oil spill in the sea. They think about the birds and fishes and mammals and plants that will die and about beaches with tarry sands.

They know that from Earth the atmosphere seems to be boundless, an ocean of air that we take for granted and breathe without thinking about it. From space they see that the atmosphere is only a thin shell surrounding the earth. Just before sunrise and just after sunset they can see it—the red layer is the air we breathe; above it is the stratosphere; the blue layer is the ionosphere. Beyond the shell is space, black and empty.

Space travelers often return with their thinking changed. On Earth we think of boundaries. The view from space is different. Rivers meander or rush from country to country without stopping, on their way to the sea. Forests reach from one country into another.

Sand and dust from the Sahara spread across the Atlantic (left) and blow toward the Americas. Smoke travels hundreds of miles on the winds. An ocean stretches from continent to continent, and the same waters wash the shores of both.

Space travelers see that the earth is one planet, small and fragile, wondrous and lovely. It is the spaceship in which we journey around the sun, and our life-support system is its air and waters and lands. We are all, every person in the world, aboard the same ship. And so we must all, in ways large and small, treasure and protect it.

· GLOSSARY ·

Definitions refer to the way terms are used in this book.

altimeter   An instrument used to measure the height of an airplane or spacecraft above the surface of the earth.

Apollo   U.S. program of manned space flights, 1968–72, that prepared for and made trips to the moon.

astronaut   The name used for a person who has flown in space aboard a U.S. craft.

atmosphere   The shell of gases surrounding the earth.

atoll   A ringlike coral and sand island surrounding a body of water known as a lagoon.

bedrock   Solid rock found beneath soil or windblown sand.

carbon dioxide   A gas in Earth's atmosphere that traps much of the sun's heat and keeps it from escaping into space.

chlorofluorocarbons (CFCs)   A group of widely used man-made gases that appear to be weakening a layer of the atmosphere that shields the earth from harmful radiation from the sun.

climate   Average weather conditions over a long period of time.

corals   Tiny sea animals with hard skeletons on the outside of their bodies, which live in colonies. Their skeletons form coral reefs.

crust   The solid, rocky outer shell of the earth.

delta   Land built from sediment carried by a river and deposited at its mouth.

desert   A mostly barren region where little rain falls.

dune   A build-up of windblown sand that usually has a gentle upwind side and a steep far side.

eddy   A swirling ring of water thrown off by a current in the ocean.

eye (of a storm)   The roughly circular area of light winds and fair weather found at the center of a hurricane or typhoon.

false-color image   A picture in which false colors have been used instead of natural ones to highlight details and to show what the unaided eye cannot see.

flood plain   The area bordering a stream, over which water spreads during a flood.

greenhouse effect   A term meaning that the earth's atmosphere traps heat from the sun in much the same way that the glass in a greenhouse does.

Gulf Stream   A warm ocean current that flows north along the eastern coast of North America and then across the North Atlantic.

hurricane   A severe, swirling, tropical storm in the North Atlantic Ocean, Caribbean Sea, Gulf of Mexico, or North Pacific Ocean off the western coast of Mexico.

iceberg   A large chunk of ice that has broken off polar land ice into the sea.

image   A picture, usually formed by a computer using information from electronic sensors or radar.

infrared   Color and heat beyond red that the unaided eye cannot detect.

Kelvin   A temperature scale that begins at absolute zero, the point at which no heat is given off, and goes up. Water freezes at 273 degrees Kelvin and boils at 373 degrees.

lagoon   A body of salty water separated from the sea by a coral reef.

Landsat   A series of unmanned U.S. satellites that orbit the earth and gather information based on visible and infrared radiation.

lava   Molten rock that wells up from inside the earth and hardens on Earth's surface.

meteorite   Any natural object from space that passes through the atmosphere without burning up and reaches Earth's surface.

Meteosat   A European weather satellite.

microwave   A form of radiation with wavelengths that are longer than those of infrared and shorter than those of shortwave radio.

Mid-Atlantic Ridge   A range of undersea mountains that runs down the middle of the Atlantic Ocean. It is a place where plates of the earth's crust pull away from each other and molten rock wells up from inside the earth.

orbit   The path followed by an object around a body such as Earth under the influence of gravity.

ozone layer   A thin layer of gas in the upper atmosphere that shields Earth from harmful rays of the sun.

plates   The big pieces of Earth's crust, which are in motion.

pollution   The dirtying of air, water, or soil by wastes.

radar   A way of sending out microwaves and radio waves and using their echoes to detect and make images of distant objects.

radiation   The sending out of waves of energy, such as light and heat.

radio waves   A form of energy with longer wavelengths than microwaves.

rain forest   Dense growth of trees in very wet climates.

remote sensing   Any means of collecting information about a target without touching it. Photography is one such means.

satellite   An object that follows a path around a body such as the sun or the earth, held there by gravitational pull.

sea ice   Ice that is frozen seawater.

Seasat   An unmanned U.S. satellite launched in 1978.

sediment   Soil and particles of rock carried by moving water.

sensor   Electronic device that detects visible and invisible radiation from the earth.

shuttle   Manned spacecraft flown by the U.S. beginning in the 1980s.

Skylab   An Earth-orbiting U.S. workshop that housed three crews in 1973 and 1974.

spectral signature   The place in the spectrum that serves to identify each kind of plant or mineral, just as a fingerprint serves to identify a person.

spectrum   Often used to mean the range of colors that can be seen by the unaided human eye, as arranged by wavelength; violet has the shortest wavelength and red the longest. Also used to mean the entire range of electric and magnetic radiation—the electromagnetic spectrum: gamma rays, X rays, ultraviolet rays, visible light rays, infrared, microwaves, and radio waves.

trench   Place in the ocean floor where two plates meet and one turns down and slides under the other.

typhoon   Severe, swirling, tropical storm of the Western Pacific.

ultraviolet rays   Radiation from the sun with wavelengths shorter than violet, which is harmful to life in large amounts.

volcano   An opening in the earth's crust where molten rock from inside the earth comes to the surface. Also, a mountain built by eruptions of such rock.

wavelength   The distance from the crest of one wave to the crest of the next. In radio waves there may be miles between one crest and the next. Red light has about 33,000 wave crests to an inch.

weather   The state of the atmosphere at any one time and place, including temperature, moisture, wind, and so on. You could live in a place with a warm, dry climate where, on a given day, the weather was cool and rainy.

· FURTHER READING ·

*indicates a young people's book.

Allen, Joseph C., with Russell Martin. *Entering Space*. New York: Stewart, Tabori, and Chang, 1984. Photographic account of astronauts in orbit.

Hitchcock, Barbara, comp. *Sightseeing: A Space Panorama*. New York: Knopf, 1986. Photographs from the U.S. space program.

Kelley, Kevin W., ed. *The Home Planet*. Reading, Mass.: Addison Wesley, 1988. A beautiful picture book with quotations from space travelers.

Kerrod, Robin. *NASA Views of Earth*. New York: Gallery Books, 1985. A well-illustrated general account.

*McGowen, Tom. *Album of Spaceflight*. New York: Macmillan, 1987. Photographs from space.

National Geographic. *Atlas of North America*. Washington, D. C., 1985. A space-age portrait of North America, with maps, images from space, and text.

*Ride, Sally, with Susan Okie. *To Space and Back*. New York: Lothrop, 1986. An astronaut tells what it's like in space.

Schick, Ron, and Julia Van Haaften, comps. *The View from Space*. New York: Potter, 1988. American astronaut photography from the years 1962–72.

Sheffield, Charles. *Earth Watch*. New York: Macmillan, 1981.

———. *Man on Earth*. New York: Macmillan, 1983. Two beautiful books for those seriously wishing to learn more about the interpretation of Landsat photographs.

· INDEX ·